Here in Britain, hedges are a permanent feature of our landscape, and we take them very much for granted. But every hedge is a little world in itself, providing most of the necessities of life for the birds, plants and animals that live within its protection. Nowadays the hedge itself needs our protection, for present-day herbicides, insecticides and farming methods are endangering its life. This book will show you just what we are in danger of losing if our hedges are destroyed.

Hedges

written and illustrated by
John Leigh-Pemberton

Ladybird Books Loughborough

THE BEGINNING

The first farmers came to Britain from the continent in about 4000 BC. These Stone Age (Neolithic) people used flint and bone tools and understood the use of fire. The small, savage population they absorbed or replaced had been chiefly hunters and gatherers of wild vegetable food.

The colonists brought with them sheep, goats, cattle and dogs which were about the size of a terrier, but they did not bring horses with them.

Ditch, bank and stockade-Neolithic man's way of forming enclosures to protect his livestock

Antlers of giant deer
(Megaloceros),
with 3 metre (10 ft) antler spread.
Still found in Britain in Neolithic times,
its antlers could be used as a digging tool

They cleared parts of the uplands of southern Britain by burning the woodland which, at that time, covered very large areas. Here they made camps in which they kept their sheep and cattle.

These camps were surrounded by a series of ditches about 2½ metres (8 ft) deep, the soil from which formed banks which were in turn surmounted by stockades of wooden stakes. These barriers were necessary in order to protect the livestock from the wild predatory mammals living in Britain at that time.

Neolithic man's dog
was probably used as a guard
and even for herding.
Complete skeletons
have been found

*The Lynx may have survived
in Britain until about
the 10th century AD.
It still survives
on the continent of Europe*

The animals from which early man had to protect himself and his herds were chiefly the Bear, Wolf and Lynx. The Fox and the Wild Cat, too, were quite common. Crops of wheat and flax also had to be protected from the huge and ferocious Aurochs, from Giant Deer, Elk and Wild Boar. All these animals have gradually died out in Britain, but many persisted into medieval and even later times when farming was far more extensive.

*The Wild Boar survived
in northern Britain
until the beginning
of the 18th century*

*The last British Wolf was killed
in the 18th century, probably in Wales.
In England the Wolf had gone
by the 16th century*

The stockades behind which man kept his livestock must gradually have become easier to make and more effective as time went on. At some point in history boughs cut from thorn trees were introduced to reinforce the timber fences, for they would have helped to keep out some of the smaller predators. It was from this ancestry that the hedge was created.

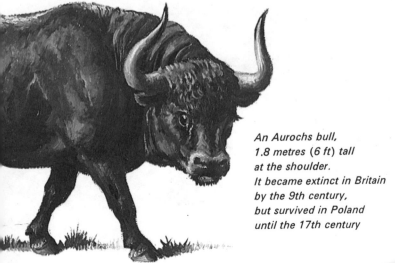

*An Aurochs bull,
1.8 metres (6 ft) tall
at the shoulder.
It became extinct in Britain
by the 9th century,
but survived in Poland
until the 17th century*

'OPEN-FIELD' FARMING

In Saxon and medieval times the land was farmed by what is called the 'open-field' method. This meant that a village would have a plot of land, cleared from the forest, which was worked more or less communally by the peasants.

The 'open-field' would be divided into strips, separated by grass borders, each strip being one *furrow* long: a furrow was reckoned as 220 yards (201 metres), hence the term 'furlong'.

THE ENCLOSURE ACTS

Gradually the 'open-field' system died out as more and more land was taken over by landlords and surrounded by hedges. This, on the whole, made for improved farming at a time when an increasing population demanded that more food should be grown.

In 1760, and thereafter until the middle of the nineteenth century, Acts of Parliament called 'Enclosure Acts' were passed which meant that many more hedges were planted. The result is the English landscape – a patchwork of hedged fields.

Hawthorn ('May')
The branches form a criss-cross mass
which, with the sharp spines,
form a very efficient barrier.
The flowers can be pink or white

THE MATERIALS OF THE HEDGE

A hedge bordering a field is usually combined with a ditch, the soil from which forms a little bank on which the hedge grows. The ditch serves to carry away surplus water from the fields, making it easier to work them.

Beech
This grows mostly
on chalky soil.
A beech hedge will keep
its brown leaves
through the winter.
The nuts are called
'beechmast'

Blackthorn
The thorns are very sharp
and the branches form
a dense mass.
The flowers bloom
before the leaves appear.
The bitter fruit
is the 'sloe'

The plants most favoured for making a hedge are the Hawthorn, Blackthorn, Holly and Beech. All these are tough and hardy. The Hawthorn is often called the 'Quick' (or 'living') thorn as opposed to the cut boughs of dead thorn used in ancient times.

Holly is evergreen
and therefore
makes a thick hedge
all through the year.
The wood is hard
and the leaves are
leathery and prickly

English Elm
A useful tree
which sends out
shoots from
its roots

MORE HEDGEROW SHRUBS

Some other shrubs find their way into hedges, sometimes accidentally and not always welcome. Elm is useful because its shoots strengthen a hedge, but Ash is a greedy plant which takes too much nourishment out of the ground.

Hazel is often found in hedges, and its nuts attract many animals. Dogwood appears on chalk, producing bitter berries with hard seeds. Hornbeam was once common in southern England, but is less so now. It is often mistaken for Beech.

Ash
Not always welcome

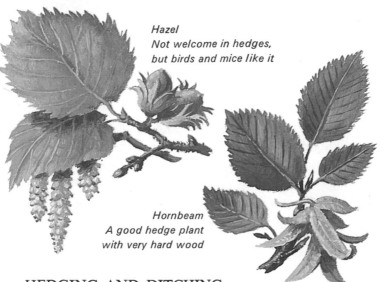

Hazel
Not welcome in hedges,
but birds and mice like it

Hornbeam
A good hedge plant
with very hard wood

HEDGING AND DITCHING

Hedges and their ditches
have to be cared for, and this
is a skilled craft. Ditches must
be cleaned out and free of
debris, and hedges must be
kept trimmed and cut back to
produce strong growth. Some
hedges are combined with
posts and rails, while others,
sadly, are repaired with barbed
wire.

Dogwood
Its wood is tough

HOW THE HEDGE BENEFITS FARMING

As well as making a visible and lasting boundary to a piece of land, hedges and ditches provide a practical way of dividing it up so that it may be used efficiently.

Livestock can be pastured safely and prevented from straying or encroaching upon grain or root crops.

Hedges provide shelter for crops and livestock from wind and snow, and these 'wind-breaks' prevent the *erosion* (wearing away) of the valuable top soil.

*The dust cloud formed by soil erosion,
caused by wind blowing
across a hedgeless landscape*

Too often in recent times long-established hedges have been removed in order to make possible the use of large farm machinery.

This has led to disastrous erosion of the irreplaceable top-soil and has done much to destroy for ever the special character of our landscape.

Ditches keep the land drained, making it possible to farm it without damage – for using tractors on soft or muddy ground can do it great harm.

The flowers and leaves in a hedge attract many kinds of butterflies such as this Small White

HOW THE HEDGE BENEFITS WILD LIFE

Hedges offer a habitat to many kinds of wild creatures. The solid structure of the hedge itself is an excellent place for many kinds of birds to nest and also affords them protection.

The insects and seeds found in hedges and ditches provide food for birds and small mammals, and the bank upon which the hedge is planted, being made up of soft soil, is very suitable for those mammals which live and breed in burrows.

Partridges like to nest in the shelter of hedges

The Sparrow Hawk
hunts along a hedgerow
for birds and
small mammals

The ditch, too, provides an easy source of water and attracts to it various forms of life such as water plants, frogs and newts.

Many hedges are very old, some as much as two hundred years, and their very permanence has made them most attractive to species which would not find homes in open ground or woodland.

Creatures living in hedgerows attract in turn the predators which hunt them.

Rabbits make their burrows
in the hedge-bank's soft soil

HEDGEROW FLOWERS

In the following pages are just a few of the common hedgerow flowers.

Honeysuckle, flowers June to September, climbs through the hedge and is very attractive to moths, who pollinate it. Flowers open fully at night

Bindweed, flowers June to October, twines anti-clockwise round other plants. The flowers close at night but open in moonlight

Flowers favour hedges because they gain protection from severe weather and can establish themselves undisturbed.

Some grow in hedges, some in the hedge bank, others in the ditch and others climb through the hedge itself.

A flower's presence in a hedge depends upon the type of soil and the locality. For instance, some flowers are found only in southern England and others only in the north. Some flowers like clay soil, others chalk or peat.

Dog Rose,
flowers June to August.
Hips (berries) in winter provide food
for mice and some birds.
Grows through the hedge

Bramble,
flowers June to
September, after which
the berries provide food
for birds, insects and
many mammals – even Foxes.
There are about 400 varieties
in Britain

THE PARSLEY FAMILY

Hemlock, flowers June to September. The leaves are very poisonous. It has a hollow stem which is spotted purple and can grow to 1.8 metres (6 ft). It has a strong, unpleasant smell. Likes damp site

Cow Parsley, flowers in April until June. Other similar plants are Chervil, Hogweed, Sweet Cicely and Stone Parsley

Hedge Parsley, a tall plant which flowers later than the others. Leaves and seeds give clues to which kind it is

This group of plants contains many species, all somewhat alike and all with fern-like leaves.

PLANTS AT RISK

Plants like these are too often dug up and transplanted to gardens. If this happens the colony of wild plants may eventually die out. Thus the hedge will be deprived of one of its great attractions.

Primrose, flowers from March to May. Primroses are full of nectar and so very much visited by bees, which pollinate them. Slightly scented

Common Forget-me-not, flowers through summer. There are ten kinds of Forget-me-nots found from streams to mountains

Sweet Violet, flowers in April. It is fragrant and likes chalk soil. A white variety is found in S.W. Britain. Nine species in all

Tufted Vetch,
flowers through
the summer.
One of many from
the large Pea family.
Climbs through
and over hedges

Wood Anemone, flowers
March and April
in great profusion
in woods as well as
hedges. There are
rare blue or lilac varieties

Scarlet Pimpernel,
flowers all summer.
They close in cloud or rain.
Many other names –
Shepherd's Sundial,
Shepherd's Clock,
Wink-a-peep,
Poor Man's Weatherglass

Black Bryony,
flowers May and June.
Our only member
of the Yam family.
It climbs by twining
clockwise through
a hedge.
The tuberous root
and berries
are poisonous

...op. flowers
...ly and August.
...und mostly in
...uthern England and used in
...ewing to add bitter flavour
...d to check fermentation.
...ltivated hops are picked
...September and October.
...is a vigorous climber

Germander Speedwell,
flowers March to August.
One of the many kinds
of Speedwells which belong
to the same family as
the Snap-dragon and Foxglove

Harebell,
flowers in dry places
July to September.
This is the English
name for
the Bluebell
of Scotland.
Note three kinds
of leaves

23

*Elder, flowers in May to July.
It prefers chalk soil.
Wine and jelly can be made
from berries, which have a
nasty taste when raw*

*Guelder Rose,
flowers in June
and July. Grows best
in damp hedgerows.
Note two sorts of flowers
– only the smaller ones
are fertile*

ACCIDENTALS

Many shrubs arrive in a hedge by accident. Although they may not strengthen the hedge they add to its attractiveness, providing nectar and fruit for insects and birds.

*Ivy, flowers very late
in October and November.
Climbs over and
through hedge
but does not harm
the tree or shrub
which supports it.
Evergreen
with two sorts of leaves*

Lords and Ladies or Cuckoo-pint, flowers in April to June, the leaf appearing early. Flies are trapped by the hairy male flowers just below the 'club'. Berries are poisonous

Hedge Bedstraw, a trailing plant which flowers in July. The stems have bristles which enable it to cling to its host

Woody Nightshade or Bittersweet, a near relative of the potato. Flowers from June until August, after which the berries appear. Poisonous for us, but birds eat them

Hedges are particularly good places for plants which like sheltered or shady situations. The three plants shown here grow in woodland as well as in a hedge.

Buttercup, flowers through spring and summer. There are about a dozen species of Buttercup in Britain.

Herb Robert is a member of the Geranium family and flowers from May to September. The flowers hang their heads in rain and at night

These are typical hedgerow flowers. Like most other plants, they vanish if the hedges are destroyed.

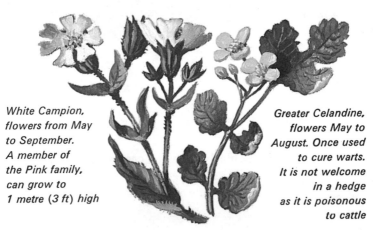

White Campion, flowers from May to September. A member of the Pink family, can grow to 1 metre (3 ft) high

Greater Celandine, flowers May to August. Once used to cure warts. It is not welcome in a hedge as it is poisonous to cattle

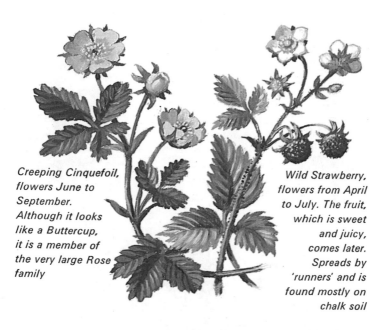

Creeping Cinquefoil, flowers June to September. Although it looks like a Buttercup, it is a member of the very large Rose family

Wild Strawberry, flowers from April to July. The fruit, which is sweet and juicy, comes later. Spreads by 'runners' and is found mostly on chalk soil

And the insects and birds which depend on them for food will disappear from the area also.

Broad-leaved Dock, flowers from July to October. It is a persistent weed. Its leaves can be 30 cm (1 ft) long and were once used as a wrap to keep butter cool

27

These three plants
belong to the 'Dead Nettle' family
which includes various kinds of Mint.
Harmless, they are no relation to
the Stinging Nettle
in spite of the name.
  Left – Betony
  Right – Black Horehound
  Below – Ground Ivy
  All flower all summer

Stinging Nettle,
flowers June
to September.
A very tough plant.
Grows in clumps
('beds').
The young shoots
can be cooked
and many butterflies
lay eggs on the leaves.
If stung apply
a wet Dock leaf

Traveller's Joy or Old Man's Beard, flowers July, then 'beards' in Autumn. A member of the Buttercup family which festoons some hedges on chalky soil in southern England

Fuchsia, flowers from June onwards into autumn. Grows in hedges in S.W. England and in W. Ireland, and on moors in Orkney. Not common but spectacular

Spindle, flowers in May and June. It is a shrub which is found on chalk soil. The fruit is poisonous, splitting open to reveal the seeds

THREE WELCOME ACCIDENTALS

The flowers which grow in hedges bordering roads are particularly at risk because herbicides are sometimes used to clear the grass verges. In this way many colonies of flowers can be destroyed for ever.

HEDGEROW INSECTS

Plants growing in a hedge attract many insects.
Various kinds of bees seek out the *nectar* (a sugary juice)
from the flowers, thus pollinating the flowers they visit.

Honey Bee (worker)

Green Hairstreak Butterfly
(*female*)

*Hedge Brown
Butterfly* (*female*)

Bramble

Many moths and butterflies do the same, laying their eggs on the leaves or stems of special flowers or grasses on which the caterpillars, when hatched, will feed.

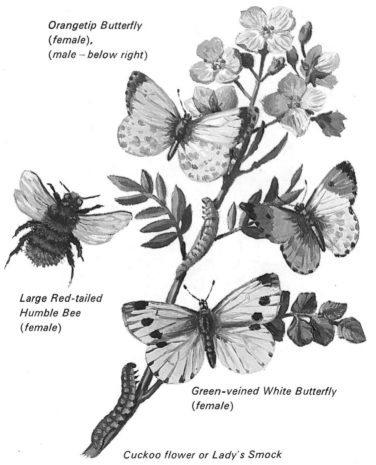

Orangetip Butterfly
(*female*),
(*male – below right*)

Large Red-tailed
Humble Bee
(*female*)

Green-veined White Butterfly
(*female*)

Cuckoo flower or Lady's Smock

Moths usually fly and feed at night, so flowers which open at dusk, such as Honeysuckle (p. 18) are pollinated by Hawk Moths who come to feed on the nectar from the flowers.

Broadbordered
Bee Hawk Moth

Small Tortoiseshell Butterfly
(female)

Peacock Butterfly
(female)

Stinging Nettles attract many species of butterflies who lay their eggs on them.

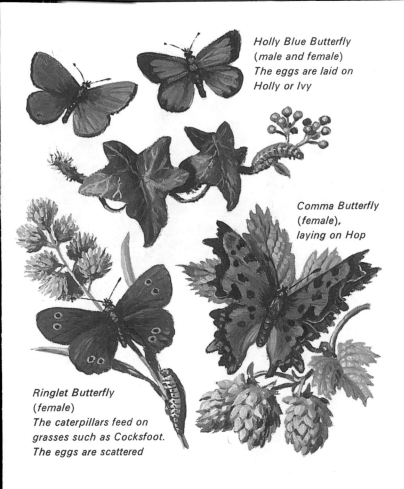

*Holly Blue Butterfly
(male and female)
The eggs are laid on
Holly or Ivy*

*Comma Butterfly
(female),
laying on Hop*

*Ringlet Butterfly
(female)
The caterpillars feed on
grasses such as Cocksfoot.
The eggs are scattered*

Some species of butterflies have declined through the destruction of their habitat. When hedges, flowers and trees are destroyed the butterflies have nowhere to feed or breed.

33

*Great Tit,
eats seeds, fruit and insects*

*Goldcrest,
eats spiders and insects*

HEDGEROW BIRDS

Shelter, nesting sites, food and drink – the hedgerow provides all these for many birds.

*Long-tailed Tit,
eats insects, spiders and
some seeds and buds*

Dunnock, or Hedge Sparrow
(*it is not a Sparrow*),
eats seeds in winter,
insects in summer

Blue Tit,
eats mostly insects

Many species which do not normally frequent hedges
will also use them occasionally for shelter or food.

Wren,
feeds on insects
and spiders

Blackbird (male),
the female is brown.
Eats insects,
fruit and seeds.
Sings from perch

Song Thrush,
eats worms, snails
and some seeds

Robin,
eats mostly insects
but also seeds and berries.
Sings in winter and summer

Its stout structure and thorny twigs make the hedge a perfect site for birds which nest in bushes rather than in trees or upon the ground. The hedge also provides a perch from which to sing.

FINCHES

Most Thrushes and Finches are apt to build in hedges, either high up or close to the ground. When the hedge is in full leaf, their nests are very well hidden.

Greenfinch,
eats mostly seeds.
The young are fed on insects.
Sings from high perch

Bullfinch (*male*),
the hen is brown.
Eats seeds, buds
and berries

Chaffinch (*male*),
the hen is duller.
Eats seeds and
a few insects

Linnet (left) and Yellowhammer (below), both typical hedgerow birds whose diet consists mainly of seeds

Although well-kept hedges are what the farmer prefers, to birds the extra height and density of an overgrown hedge is very attractive.

There will be more seeds, berries and insects in such a hedge, and therefore a better supply of food and a wider choice of nesting sites.

*Turtle Dove (left)
and Whitethroat (right),
two summer visitors
which frequent hedges*

Every spring migrant birds come to us from as far away as Asia and Africa in order to breed. Many of them find sanctuary in our hedges, where they can nest and feed their young.

These visitors are already becoming fewer, and will continue to do so if their chosen habitat is destroyed.

*The Little Owl
was introduced into Britain
from Holland in 1889.
Only 21.5 cm (8½ in) long.
It often hunts by day*

Hornbeam twig

Insects, birds and small mammals which occupy a particular habitat will attract to it those other creatures which prey on them.

Among bird predators the Sparrow Hawk, Little Owl and Magpie are keen hunters along a hedge. The Sparrow Hawk and Little Owl will take insects, small birds and mammals; the Magpie robs nests of the eggs and young of other birds.

Branch of
Field Maple

Magpie,
a member of the Crow family
and, like them, very intelligent.
It will eat almost anything

Magpies are not the only nest robbers. Egg collectors may deprive a bird of its eggs and in doing so may scare it from its habitat. Most birds in Britain are protected by Acts of Parliament and it is illegal to take a protected bird or its eggs.

So 'bird-nesting' is not only cruel, damaging and pointless – it can also be against the law and punishable by a fine.

HEDGEROW MAMMALS

Harvest Mouse,
here shown life-size.
This is Britain's smallest rodent,
now somewhat reduced in numbers in some areas.
Lives in burrows in winter but in nest built in grass,
crops or hedge in summer.
Eats mostly grain and berries, some insects.
Lives about 18 months. Almost odourless

The soil from which a hedge bank is made is usually that taken from the ditch. This soil is softer, looser and less compacted than that of the surrounding area. It is therefore of great advantage to mammals which make burrows, such as mice and rabbits.

Wood Mouse,
or Long-tailed Field Mouse,
87 mm (3.4 in) long
with a tail about the same.
Lives and breeds in burrows
where food is also stored.
Eats grain, seeds, nuts,
sometimes snails, insects.
Bigger ears and eyes
than House Mouse (below)

House Mouse.
It originated in Asia
and spread into Europe
in pre-historic times.
Now world-wide
and very destructive.
It will live in hedgerows
as well as in ricks and houses.
79 mm (3.1 in) long
and tail 77 mm (3 in)

As well as being made of soft soil the hedge bank, being raised above the surrounding area, tends to be better drained. This, combined with the protection of the hedge itself and the variety of food readily available, makes the hedge bank a very desirable habitat.

*Rabbit, 40 cm (16 in) long,
it was introduced into Britain by the Normans
but came originally from Spain*

*Rabbits eat huge amounts of vegetable matter
and do great damage to crops. They can breed all the year*

Rabbits live in *warrens* which are made up of a series of burrows, some complicated and some merely short tunnels. A large hedge bank would be needed to accommodate a warren and the hedge is not the only habitat for rabbits. They will establish themselves in a wide variety of habitats from woodland to mountains or sand dunes.

Foxes, badgers, stoats, rats and even cats will share a warren with rabbits.

Modern farming methods which involve the destruction of small copses and hedges have certainly contributed to the decrease in the population of Dormice in this century.

In summer Dormice build nests above ground for sleeping and breeding and will build them in a hedge if it contains Honeysuckle for nesting material and hazel and beech for food.

Dormouse, 75 mm (3 in) long, with a furry tail a little shorter. Dormice are nocturnal and one of the few British mammals which hibernate. They eat nuts and seeds

Hedgehog,
23 cm (9 in) long,
eats worms, slugs, beetles, berries.
Rolls into a prickly ball
to defend itself
but Foxes can kill it
quite easily.
Nocturnal, but active
at dawn and dusk.
In winter it
hibernates

IN THE HEDGE-BOTTOM

Where the bank and hedge meet is called the *hedge-bottom*. Here grass, dead leaves and twigs collect, especially in neglected hedges, and this litter makes a habitat for some mammals.

Hedgehogs spend the winter in leafy nests, hibernating in a hedge-bottom.

Water Shrew,
85 mm (3.3 in) long
with tail of 61 mm (2.4 in).
Lives largely in water,
feeding on small fish
as well as snails and insects.
Sometimes found far from
water. Like all Shrews,
bitter tasting, but Owls and
large fish will eat them

Common Shrew,
75 mm (3 in) long
with a tail of 38 mm (1.5 in).
A very small but very fierce little
animal which lives for only about a year.
Shrews have very fragile bones and may die
of shock if handled. Eats worms and beetles

The same sorts of conditions are favoured by shrews, of which there are five kinds in Britain. Bank Voles may be found there, too, while Water Shrews may sometimes use a clear ditch.

Bank Vole,
95 mm (3.7 in) long
plus 50 mm (2 in) tail.
Eats berries, insects
and toadstools.
Makes tunnels in long
grass or hedge litter.
Can climb well
in search of food.
Active mostly by day.
Makes nest for
breeding

MAMMAL PREDATORS

The fact that a hedge harbours animals like mice, rabbits and voles ensures that other animals which prey on them will search for them there.

Thus Stoats and Weasels, which live principally on small rodents and rabbits as well as on young birds and their eggs, will frequent hedgerows, hunting by day.

Stoat,
28 cm (11 in) long
plus tail 11 cm (4.3 in).
The male is much larger than
the female and newborn young
have fine white hair.
Stoats moult twice a year,
turning white in winter
in northern part of their range
when they are called ermine

Weasel,
20 cm (8 in) long
plus a 6 cm (2.3 in) tail.
The males are very much bigger
than the females. Weasels are
so small that they can follow
a mouse down its hole.
They lack the Stoat's dark tip
to the tail

Both the Stoat and the Weasel are highly efficient hunters able to run surprisingly fast for animals with such short legs. They can also climb, jump (Stoat's long jump 2.5 m – 8 ft), and swim easily and well.

Prey is killed by a bite at the back of the neck. Hunting is often carried out by family parties.

Fox,
65 cm (2 ft 2 in) long
plus a tail (brush) *40 cm (16 in).*
Mostly nocturnal and solitary
except in the breeding season.
Highly intelligent, a Fox can
swim well and will climb trees
when hunted.
Mostly carnivorous
but will eat fruit
and insects

Foxes will use a hedge and its ditch as a hunting ground or as cover as they stalk rabbits or birds feeding out in a field. They may sometimes take over a rabbit's burrow as their *earth*.

Provided that it is on sandy soil, a badger will take over or even share a rabbit's warren in a hedge; and as a hedge provides a wide variety of food, the omnivorous badger will visit it in search of worms and berries as well as mice and young rabbits.

Badger,
92 cm (3 ft) long
including tail 10 cm (4 in).
Nocturnal, and in winter
will spend days on end
asleep – but no hibernation.
Makes huge and
complicated sets (burrows)
in wide variety of habitats.
Lives with family
for most of the year.
Immensely strong,
inquisitive
and playful

THE HEDGE, A SUMMARY

The hedge, then, fulfils a wide variety of functions. It has practical uses for farming and is largely responsible for the unique appearance of much of our landscape.

Protecting the soil, it offers at the same time habitat for wild life in a complete food chain. The plants grow because of the conditions the hedge offers; the insects depend on the plants and the birds on the plants and the insects. And the mammals depend upon the whole small world which the hedge provides.

INDEX